I0075077

Why I Should Write a Book

The Smart Entrepreneur's Secret to Massive Leverage and Growth

Osamede Arhunmwunde

Couronne Publishing
Winnipeg, Manitoba

Copyright © 2016 –Osamede Arhunmwunde.

All rights reserved. No part of this publication may be repro-
duced, distributed or transmitted in any form or by any means,
including photocopying, recording, or other electronic or me-
chanical methods, without the prior written permission of the
publisher, except in the case of brief quotations embodied in crit-
ical reviews and certain other noncommercial uses permitted by
copyright law. For permission requests, write to the publisher,
addressed "Attention: Permissions Coordinator," at the address
below:

Couronne Publishing Inc.
3377 Pembina Highway,
Winnipeg, MB. Canada
R3V1A2
Info@couronnepublishing.com
www.couronnepublishing.com

Ordering Information:
Quantity sales. Special discounts are available on quantity pur-
chases by corporations, associations, and others. For details, contact the "Special Sales Department" at the address above.

Why I Should Write A Book –Osamede Arhunmwunde
-1st edition.
ISBN 978-0-9948637-5-1

CONTENTS

This book is dedicated to God almighty; without Him I would be lost. To my parents Mr. & Mrs. B.O. Arhunmwunde, for their sacrifices, unwavering love and support all through the years. To my beautiful wife Chansa for her love and support even when the "going gets tough". To Mubarak Nsekarije, my "work out partner" for his commitment to success and all the sleepless nights and sacrifices to ensure that we live an extraordinary life filled with purpose. To Chidi Ajaere, for having faith in me. Happiness is a friend who has become a brother. I truly stand on the shoulders of giants. Thank you for being part of my story.

As a special bonus for readers of this book, I'm offering you access to our advanced Authorship Webinar for Entrepreneurs and Business Professionals

Introducing:
"How to Easily Write, Publish and Use a Book to Grow Your Business, and Earn a Fortune"

At the end of this book, I'll tell you how you can gain access absolutely FREE

Introduction

Did you know that by choosing to be a published author, you have joined an elite group that forms 1% of the global population?

So many people around the world want to write a book, estimates suggest about 80% of North Americans want to write a book but only about 1% actually writes and publishes a book. When you take a look at the number of published authors around the world and compare it to the world's population you can see that 1% trend appearing again.

Why is there such a disparity between those who want to write a book and those who actually do write a book?

It is because most people like the idea and perks of becoming an author but they believe subconsciously that they can't actually become one. They believe for an equally strange reason that Authors are special people with special skills. And there lies your opportunity. That belief is what makes an Author "special" in the subconscious mind of most individuals. Choosing to become an author sets you apart from your competition in a unique way. It puts you in a place of Authority.

Why should you write a book?

That's a fair question to ask, one that I will explore with you throughout this book.

Out of curiosity who would you rather do business with; the man who hands you a business card on marketing or the Author who hands you his book on marketing?

One thing is certain; the business card would end up in the trash faster than the book. As individuals we have been taught to place a high value on a book. We do not put books in the trash –that has been engraved in our subconscious minds from a young age. We place books on a shelf, on the carved mantle above the fireplace for all to see.

We go to books for solutions and or entertainment. This is why the world for good reasons, view authors as experts.

I once read a quote by Chuck Palahniuk:

"We all die.
The goal isn't to live forever;
the goal is to create something that will."

Now I can give you a dozen reasons why you should publish a book, but above everything else, a published book gives you a chance for immortality. Just think about it.

If you died today, what evidence is there of the life you lived, your challenges and victories, your beliefs and visions, your Legacy?

What is there for the world to remember you?

A book will outlive you. A book can be a record of your life. It is a mark on the sands of time that you were here.

"Somethings don't last forever, but somethings do. Like a good song, or a good book, or a good memory you can take out and unfold in your darkest times..."

- Sarah Dessen

My name is Osamede Arhunmwunde and I am an international best-selling author. We can at least agree on how powerful and credible that sounds for a start. I haven't always been a success-ful author! I went from dreaming about "I want to write a book" to "I have written and published a book" and a whole new world of opportunities opened up to me.

My books have been in more countries that I could have ever hoped for. My books have been into homes that I would otherwise have not been welcomed into. My books now form a huge part of the marketing piece for my business. And my income has grown astronomically as a result of writing a book.

Writing a book has got to be one of my life's greatest achievement for all it has brought into my life. My desire is for you to find your reason within the words in this book and experience all of the joy that comes from becoming an author.

[2]

The Best
Vs
The Best Known

Life is a study; to be successful, you must study success. Look closely at the most successful people in your field, and you'll discover something amazing—these people aren't necessarily the most talented or the best. They are just the best-known.

Is Dr. Oz the best doctor?
Is T. Harv Eker the best wealth adviser?
Is Dr. Phil the best psychologist?
Is Suze Orman the best personal finance guru?

I don't think so!

There are many people who can do what they do, and do it better.

Yet, these celebrity entrepreneurs rose to the top while others faltered.

- **What's their secret?**

- **Why do these chosen few get the most respect and the biggest incomes?**

- **How did they build their empires and rake in hundreds of times more money than their closest competitors?**

Too many young entrepreneurs think that in order to be successful, they have to put in more hours on the job, but the truth is that massive success is hardly as a result of "hard work" or the number of hours you put in. Everyone has the exact same number of hours in the day, so it can't be as the result of your "working hours". Working harder and putting in overtime can only get you so far, and it will never be enough to get you to the top.

My teacher Jim Rohn use to say:

> *"Work harder on yourself*
> *than you do on your job;*
> *work hard at your job*
> *and you can make a living.*
> *Work hard on yourself*
> *and you can make a fortune."*

Wouldn't it be great if there was a better way?
-Well, there is!

What you need is the secret that Brendon Burchard, Raymond Aaron, Dr. Phil, Suze Orman, Tony Robbins, Tim Ferriss, T. Harv Eker, David Chilton, Jack Canfield and many others have discovered, something they have that you don't...
Credibility.

WHAT IS CREDIBILITY?

Credibility is the power to inspire belief. But that's just the dictionary definition. To master the art of credibility, you must excel in these five key areas:

- Integrity
- Competence
- Sound judgment
- Empathy
- Likability

1. Having integrity means that you are honest. You demonstrate strong moral principles. Integrity goes to the heart of a person's moral character. It is a measure of their value system. A person who demonstrates great integrity is one who is living an authentic life.

2. A competent person is one who can do a task successfully and efficiently. They have mastered a talent and acquired an expertise. They have a skill

that they have honed to a fine perfection.

3. A person with sound judgment shows great intelligence and perceptiveness. They have a track record of making good decisions in the face of great complexity. They anticipate problems and make contingency plans.

4. An empathetic person can imagine themselves into the place of another person. They can mentally and emotionally "walk a mile in someone else's shoes." They are sensitive to the relationships between people. They have high emotional intelligence.

5. A likeable person is someone who demonstrates both warmth and presence. They are good listeners and pay attention to our need, not just their own. We want to be around these people, because they validate us and make us feel good about ourselves.

Expertise is also important, but it is not necessarily a core element of credibility, because many people who can inspire belief are not themselves the experts, but help us connect with those who are.

Someone like Oprah Winfrey, for example, is credible not because she knows a lot about a lot of things, but because she connects her fans with people who are true experts in their respective fields. She is not primarily known as an expert, but as a tastemaker. And because Oprah Winfrey is credible—honest, competent, intelligent, empathetic, and likeable—she inspires millions to believe.

Successful people achieve a balance between expertise and likability. We don't just want to do business with a know-it-all. We want to do business with people we like. We also want to avoid people who seem to be "fake", or wearing a mask, or just telling us what we want to hear. A likeable person can build rapport easily, and this is one of the secrets to achieving great success.

How to Gain Instant Credibility

What do Brendon Burchard, Raymond Aaron, Dr. Phil, Suze Orman, T. Harv Eker, David Chilton, Jack Canfield, Dr. Oz, Tony Robbins, and Tim Ferriss all have in common?

They've written books.

That's the real secret to gaining instant credibility: become a published author!

This is the time-tested strategy that these and many other top earners used to command respect, multiply their business, and rake in passive income, year after year.

Sure, there may be other ways to achieve the same ends, but none is as quick and effective as publishing a book with your name on it. And you don't have to be a bestseller to benefit from publishing. Just having a book with your name on it can give you a competitive advantage.

Take Suze Orman, for example. She has incredible authority in her chosen field of personal finance, and millions of loyal followers seek her out for financial advice through her books, lectures, and television appearances. She has carved out a dominant position in a very crowded market, teaching average people how they can earn, keep, and grow their money.

But how did Suze Orman earn most of her money?

By publishing books.

Now keep in mind, Suze Orman wasn't always an author. She started off as an investment consultant for Merrill Lynch and Prudential Bache Securities. Just like hundreds of other people you've never heard of. Then she decided to write and publish a book. She started small. Her first success as an author was a little booklet she wrote called The Facts on Single Premium Whole Life. At first she gave it away for free, but that one little book launched her vast media empire.

And now, according to Forbes, she's personally worth $35 million.

Not bad, eh?

BUSINESS BENEFITS OF AUTHORSHIP

Writing and publishing books not only establishes instant credibility, but offers many other business benefits. So many, in fact, those entrepreneurs who don't become authors are putting themselves at a distinct disadvantage to those who do.

The first obvious benefit is financial. Many great fortunes are built on publishing success. Suze Orman, for example, gives financial advice to average Joe but she didn't build her empire by following her own advice. Her empire is built on the back of her intellectual property -her books. Those books helped her get speaking engagements and even a popular television show. She owes her success to becoming an author.

A second benefit is authority. Having a book with your name on it gives your opinions more weight. As an author, you will be taken more seriously and you may be offered opportunities such as speaking engagements and media interviews. A book will make you an expert in the eyes of others, who will then seek out your advice, your products, and your services.

A third benefit is exposure. Putting your name on a book will get your name and face on bookshelves. Those could be physical bookshelves in stores that people walk into, or they could be virtual bookshelves like on Amazon, iBooks, Google, and Goodreads, places where millions of people browse daily when they want to solve a problem. You could be the solution to their problem, but if you're not on the bookshelf, they may never find you.

A fourth benefit is increased sales of your related products and services. Because of your book, more people will come to know and trust you, and this can accelerate your business. Readers feel a special connection to their favorite authors, and this connection will allow you to turn casual readers into repeat customers.

A fifth benefit is branding. Writing a book allows you to define yourself in the marketplace. In 1982 Martha Stewart branded herself with a book called Entertaining, and used that book and many others to launch her career. In 2000 Anthony Bourdain branded himself with a book called Kitchen Confidential: Adventures in the Culinary Underbelly, and now he has a popular cable show that allows him travel the world and explore his passions. Countless others have grown their media empires with a book as the seed.

A sixth benefit is access. Once you become a published author, a world of opportunities will open up to you. You will become a member of an elite club that includes writers and experts of every type. As an author, you can interview rich, successful, and powerful people who will be thrilled to share their expertise with you and your readers. This is what Tim Ferriss does. He's written many bestsellers by interviewing experts and sharing what he's learned. Now when Tim Ferriss reaches out to a high-powered industry leader, you can be sure they return his call.

Not yet convinced?

Then think about this: what's the difference between an author and a salesman?

When an author arrives, people line up.

When a salesman calls, people hang up.

So why not write a book, and let your pages do the selling?

PERSONAL BENEFITS OF AUTHORSHIP

Of course, not every author has a business motive for writing. For many people, money isn't everything, or even the most important thing.

Becoming an author can give you a sense of identity. It can be a form of self-discovery. It can help you define yourself to others, rather than having others define you. When I wrote my first book –Higher education 101 this was certainly the case.

Once you've written and published a book, people will look at you differently. Whether or not you become famous, you will find that others respect you more, and that you will have more influence in all areas of your life.

And of course, there is nothing to compare with the sense of accomplishment and satisfaction that comes from finishing a book and seeing it on the shelves.

[3]

Money Is Important

I've read my fair share of philosophy and we may all agree that money isn't the yardstick for all measurements; but when it's all said and done, you have to contribute your fair share to society, and for most people, they've got bills to pay, business expenses to take care of, and a family to support. Earning more money means you can support more of the things you care about.

In the words of the Zig Ziglar:

> "Money isn't everything but it ranks right up there with oxygen."

Speaking as an Economist, this is the way our world is structured: We get paid for the value we bring to the market place. In the world of authors and publishers, this payment comes in form of royalty. It's all about demand and supply. Once you can find that crowd of hungry readers, and you can supply them with your information/ knowledge/book, that's it! You can totally transform your life –Economically speaking.

Everyday people exchange money for business solutions, health solutions, wealth solutions and or entertainment. Most of these can be effectively delivered as a book.

If you want to live your life on your own terms and you are looking for the kind of job which will allow you to experience the pleasure of watching your children grow, seeing your wife evolve or maybe your parents get older and wiser, writing is definitely one of those jobs that best suits the equation. Creativity can prosper the humblest of people and situation.

I know there may be a lot of questions brimming in your mind with regards to how much money we are talking about. I heard a lot of budding writers enquire if the writing profession is good enough to allow them to quit their 9 to 5 job or if it could help them sustain their life and so on.

The answer is yes but it definitely varies from one person to another. The amount of money which you can get from the field of writing varies upon too many factors. In my publishing company for example we advise certain clients to give away their books for free. Now certainly these clients are not writing books in order to directly sell copies but to profit on the back end of the giveaway – More on this in the coming chapters. Conversely we have clients who have successfully built an impressive passive income stream with their book(s) just from the direct sales of their book.

Here are a few points to note when looking to write for front-end income:

PEOPLE WILL JUDGE YOUR BOOK BY THE COVER

If you have a poorly designed cover, good luck selling your Content!

Yes content is king, but before people get to judge your content they will judge your book cover and that can make or break the deal! Look, subconsciously people will equate the quality of your book cover to the quality of your content. As a publisher I look at dozens of book covers every day and I find it fascinating how little time some people spend in getting the right covers for their book. You can get a high quality cover today inexpensively online, but some people just don't care I suppose.

Let me break it down for you; a quality cover is proof that you've put thought and effort into the book – a good signal for a prospective buyer. You could think of your book cover like a billboard, trying to catch the attention of browsers as they speed by. Billboards usually have 6 words or less. You have to "get it" at 60 kilo meters per hour, in 3 to 5 seconds.

A book cover ought to do the same thing. At a glance your prospect ought to know;

- The genre of your book,
- The general subject matter
- Some idea of the tone or "ambiance" of the book.

Is it a motivational book? A recipe book? Or a memoir of your time in Benin City?

Each of these books needs a cover that tells at a glance what the book is about.

CONTENT IS KING

Ever wondered as to why some books sell more than the others long term?

Now long term is "the keyword". Yes in order to sell copies of your book, your book has to "look" like a bestselling book at first impression. That covers your title, book cover, description and all that "face value" the customer first sees when he or she picks up your book. Yes this can help drive the sale of your book in the short term, but you must remember that the #1 way people buy books is through referrals. So what would ensure the sale of your book in the long term?

The answer lies in the content. The content of your book is definitely "the meat", the "King of the castle", the one factor that can stand the test of time, and would ensure the success of your book in the long term. You need to be sure that your book gives something of value to the readers. By definition, Value states that the focus should be on your target readership not on you. How would your book benefit them?

It's all economics; the market place is always ready to exchange money for value. If a reader feels that he learned absolutely nothing from the book, he is least likely to recommend it to others or purchase any others book which you write - Remember word of mouth/referral is the #1 way books are sold. This is why you need to be very sure about the content. I am not just talking about the non-fiction books here. If you take a look at the fiction books as well, the content is always important.

If your plot-line is sloppy and fails to entice the readers, or you have poor character development and readers can't connect, they most likely will not read the book till the very end and they will end up having a negative mindset about your book and most importantly your brand.

A very high percentage of the books we publish in both fiction and non-fiction categories go on to become best sellers in their genre because for one, we educate our clients on delivering the best content to the market place. Remember a book is a medium to exchange an idea.

The question you want to answer clearly that your ideal readership is already asking subconsciously is this:

Why should I take time out of my busy life to read this book, when there are thousands of similar books I could read (let alone movies and shows I could be watching)?

STYLE

A writing style tells a lot about the author. When you are looking to make your books hit the bestseller list, you will have to put in a lot of emphasis on your writing style. In my opinion, the best writing style is the one which speaks to your target audience.

"You cannot boil an ocean."

When readers are connected to your writing style, they are much more likely to get hooked to your book. Now remember that your target audience "speaks a specific language". When I say "language" I am referring to "emotional language". You need to write in a style that embodies that "emotional language". When your ideal reader picks up your book, he or she needs to feel like you are speaking directly to them. They need to feel that you understand what they are going through; this will cause them to subconsciously believe you have the solution they need.

In the case of non-fiction, people are looking to escape their reality and or be entertained. They need to connect with your characters and "travel in your plot".

When you are just beginning in the field of writing, you may have to work a little on your style. If you are looking for some form of inspiration, you can always read books by other authors in your niche. Ideally bestselling books, to get an idea of what styles are getting the best results in your niche. Why bestselling books? Because "numbers don't lie".

J.K. ROWLING – THE BILLIONAIRE, THE LEGEND.

We are all aware of how J.K. Rowling became a household name. She wasn't born with a golden spoon in her mouth. We have all heard her rags to riches story. The Harry Potter saga became such an instant hit that she went on to become a billionaire. Though she had recently dropped from the billionaire list, but her success story still stands tall. Those of you who are debating whether or not writing has enough money should first go through her life journey before jumping to any conclusions.

Of course, I am well aware of the fact that not everyone can have such a prolific success record and not every book can go on to sell as many copies as the Potter series did. Still, it is an inspiring example which proves that when you are doing what you do best, the odds of making it big is surely very high.

While JK Rowling turned out to be an international best seller and her book was read by nearly everyone, there are authors who end up becoming national best sellers. These people can earn quite a lot of money too. Look at the New York best sellers list or a wide range of other lists that are announced from time to time. If you take a look at the bestsellers on online stores like Amazon, you will find that quite a lot of authors make it to this list. They too manage to make a substantial amount of money and so if you have doubted whether or not writing a book can support you to financial freedom, you need to know that it can.

I won't tell you that every author ends up being extremely successful, because that would be a lie. However, at the end of the day, writing a book will improve your income no matter what business you are associated with, period!

SMART MONEY

One of the best things about writing a good book is that it continues to pay long after you are done working on it. Remember we get paid for the value we bring to the market place. For as long as your work continues to offer value in the market place, you will continue to earn a royalty on that work.

Do you understand what a passive source of income truly is? There are a lot of people who are looking for passive income these days owing to the plethora of benefits which it has to offer. If you are not familiar with the term, it means a form of income wherein the money keeps rolling long after you have put in your efforts for the work. To make things clearer, let me give you an example.

You must have heard of Paulo Coelho, after all who hasn't! His books are such a great source of inspiration and there are various readers who have claimed that his books have shaped their approach to life. I am a huge Coelho fan myself. He wrote 'The Alchemist' long back, but even today, the royalty he gets from the book keeps rolling. This is exactly what passive income is. He doesn't need to put in any more effort for the books that have already been released, but the income keeps on rolling even now.

There are plenty of passive income opportunities and writing is the best.

[4]

Leverage

There has been a lot of doom and gloom for newly published authors since the boom of the self-publishing industry. The average authors who primarily focus their efforts on publishing books for the front end royalties are not making nearly as much money as they should. Does that mean that it's a waste of time to write a book in the first place?

Not at all! It just means that you need to take a different approach. After all, Einstein defined insanity as:

"Doing the same thing over and over again and expecting different results."

Our lesson here is that we need to avoid following the same template that most authors use.

Most people who write and publish a book are expecting to make a ton of money from royalties. Therefore, they get locked into this one goal and forget about everything else. The key is to leverage your book so that you're getting much more than just money from royalties front-end.

A book is worth so much more than the sum of its royalties. That's where so many people really drop the ball. Don't follow those same mistakes. Make sure that you have effectively leveraged your book.

DON'T FORGET TO LINK YOUR BOOK TO YOUR BUSINESS

I see books far too often that don't include a page related to the author's business. That's a cardinal sin in the world of book publishing. If you have written a book that is relevant to your business, then you have to give readers an opportunity to learn what else you can offer them.

The absolute best place to do this is at the end of the book since you have the reader's full attention. The About the Author section is a great place to start but don't be afraid to sprinkle in some bits about your business throughout the whole book. After all, there is no guarantee that they will read the About the Author section. They will read the content though.

Another powerful method of linking your book to your business is to provide bonus content on your website. Some examples you can consider might be:

- PDF Worksheets: This is my favorite option for eBooks. It's easy to provide printable worksheets on your website.

- Motivational Posters: You can design a couple of posters that readers can print/purchase and hang on their wall to help remind them of key points.

- Videos: Videos are the absolute king of media. Consider creating a few videos that illustrate key points in your book. Make these freely available and simply send readers to those videos. As an added bonus, videos can be a great method of getting people to buy your book in the first place!

- Workshop Discounts: If your business offers workshops then give readers a special offer.

Finally, any of the above methods can be offered in exchange for your readers' email addresses. This adds even more leverage to your book.

USE ENDORSEMENTS TO EXPAND YOUR REACH

One of the reasons for the decline in book sales is the fact that readers are skeptical. They are not going to be bothered to consider the pros and cons of reading your book versus someone else in your niche. That's why getting endorsements is such a big deal. It allows you to reduce buyers' uncertainty by having someone who is a recognized expert in your industry tell them that it's worth buying.

In fact, it's safe to say that endorsements are one of the best methods for getting an edge on most other authors. If an expert has taken the time to read your book, they it shows that they respect you as a professional in your niche. So it earns buyers' respect without them reading a single word of your book. If you are respected, then people are going to buy your book.

In addition to the endorsement, you can leverage it even further.

- Ask him/her to email the details of your book to their distribution list.

I recommend that you prepare the email ahead of time so all they have to do is send it.

- Exchange the endorsement for an interview. Entrepreneurs love being interviewed so many will happily accept this offer. As an added bonus, an interview will get you in front of their audience so it's a win-win situation.

- Ask him/her to share the details of your book to their followers on social media. Like with the email, I recommend that you prepare this post ahead of time so all they have to do is post it.

YOUR BOOK CAN BE USED TO GAIN NEW PROSPECTS FOR YOUR BUSINESS

Business owners spend a lot of time on potential prospects. We've all been through this drill of putting together an inquiry, going through samples to find something to send them, and providing consultations. If you keep track of how much this is costing you then you already know that it's a very high number! All of this effort doesn't even guarantee that you're going to land the prospect!

A book can be used to leverage prospects by pre-selling them on your expertise, rather than having to spend hours convincing them of your value. Simply give them a free copy of your book to read.

- It answers most of their questions.

- They learn how you work.

- They learn about your business and the systems you use.

- You earn their trust.

Using your book to presell prospects costs you around $5 and will save you countless hours of painstaking effort. Plus it increases your chances of landing that prospect.

PUTTING IT ALL TOGETHER

Publishing a book is a time-consuming process that does cost money. At first glance, the time/cost might not seem worth the number of books you will need to sell in order to make up for those costs. Don't let that discourage you. If you leverage it properly then you will more than make up for that cost.

Your book is more like a detailed business card that is used to generate leads. Royalties are simply an added bonus. Start looking at your book as a tool and leverage it rather than a product that you are going to try pushing down people's throats.

[5]

How to Get
Media Attention
In One Easy Step

One of the great challenges for any new business is getting the word out once the doors are open. Advertising and marketing can be expensive, and a new venture has no word of mouth to bring in customers.

What if there was a simple way to get free publicity for almost any product or service? Well, there is.

One of the best ways to get noticed in a crowded market is to become an author and publish a book. In addition to bringing in royalty income, increasing your credibility, establishing authority, and defining your brand, a book is a great means of generating free publicity.

This is because there is a natural, symbiotic relationship between various forms of media and book authors. Newspapers, radio and television outlets, and online venues love to feature authors, and if you position yourself correctly these media channels will jump at the chance to give you free publicity you could never afford to buy.

Think of it. How much does it cost to run a television commercial? Tens of thousands of dollars per minute, at least, even in local TV markets. And yet, a morning show might have you as a guest for fifteen minutes at no charge, and some talk shows will even pay you to appear and cover your travel and lodging expenses.

The key is that media outlets need content, which includes news and features. Local media will want local content, which is a great way to start when you're a new author.

It helps if your book is timely. If your book is related to something currently in the news, or is seasonal, or in some way captures the zeitgeist, you could use that as a hook to attract the attention of media mavens.

But evergreen topics can work just as well. Subjects like health, beauty, business, psychology and relationships are constantly in demand. A unique approach to any of these topics could be enough to get you in the door.

Once you have a book to promote, there are lots of different types of media that can give you free publicity. Let's examine a few of them.

NEWSPAPERS

This is one of the oldest and best ways to get free publicity. If your book is newsworthy, contact your local paper to set up a feature. Pretty much every newspaper these days has a website where you can find their contact method and discover how they like to be pitched.

You'll need to have a pitch ready in advance. If you're calling by phone, write out your pitch and rehearse it. This is a sales call. You need a hook that gets the editor interested in your topic. You should also have an Electronic Press Kit (EPK) on your website, with a one-sheet describing your book, plus visual material like cover art, author photo, charts, graphs, etc., depending on the nature of your book.

Another way to interest news editors is to issue a press release. There are a number of free and paid press release services online. The nice thing about a press release is you can issue one release and it will go out to dozens and maybe hundreds of editors around the country and around the world.

Of course, there's no substitute for a hands-on approach, so don't be afraid to cold call. You can also hire a PR agent, but if you're just starting out and want to keep your overhead low, you can do the leg work yourself. That way, you'll develop your own contacts and relationships with editors that can be invaluable over the course of your career.

MAGAZINES

The main differences between newspapers and magazines are their lead times, publication cycles, and sometimes the depth of their coverage. Magazines do more "think-pieces," whereas newspapers tend to be more reactive to current events. As with newspapers, you'll want to issue a press release, and also contact magazines via their website.

TELEVISION

You can approach television shows much as you would newspapers and magazines. Generally speaking, television will be harder to break into, but you shouldn't let that stop you from trying. They need content, too. And you might just have the story they need. It's usually best to start with your local stations.

You can practice your pitch, and if they bring you on, practice your television presentation. Once you get your feet wet, use the local TV clips to help land a national placement.

Radio shows

Many radio stations feature interviews with authors, especially when the topic is of timely interest or has a great hook. Because radio interviews are often conducted by phone, you can easily land interviews with stations throughout the country and throughout the world. Here, the Internet is key. Search on Google, and also on Facebook. Follow stations on Twitter. Pay attention when stations interview authors. Research other books in your field to see where they are getting exposure, and then pitch your book to those same stations.

PODCASTS

Like radio shows, podcasting is an audio format. The main difference is that podcasts are done exclusively on the web, and the episodes are archived for easy access in the future. You can approach these shows as you would a radio show. Because podcasting is still a relatively new format, you may find more opportunities with this type of media.

YOUTUBE

Many podcasts are also on YouTube. Talking head interviews may use Google Hangouts, Skype, or similar technology, and then archive the interviews on YouTube and Vimeo.

There are also YouTube-only channels that are not connected to a podcast. Search on YouTube for books in your field, and see what avenues might be available to you.

You may also want to create a simple book trailer for YouTube and Vimeo. Remember that YouTube is the biggest search engine for videos, and getting your book on YouTube can get you thousands or maybe even millions of additional hits.

BLOG TOUR INTERVIEWS

There are more than 150 million blogs on the Internet, and they all need content. Not every blog will be interested in your book, but you only need to connect with a few key influencers in your market. Some blogs focus specifically on books, and you may want to start your blog tour with these venues.

What is a blog tour? That's where you contact a series of blogs for a book promotion, usually during the launch of a new title. You then do interviews with one after another in short period of time. Because many bloggers will ask the same questions, you can reuse your answers, thought you should reword them slightly for each interview. You might also suggest questions to bloggers who may not be familiar with you and your business.

The great thing about a blog tour, as opposed to an old-fashioned book tour, is you can do it from the comfort of your home, office, or coffee shop, since the interviews are done online and usually through email.

GUEST POST ON BLOGS

In addition to Q&A style interviews, you may be able to write guests posts on blogs, and tie the subject matter to your book and your business. Having a book to talk about will give you instant credibility, and you can leverage this into publicity.

Another nice feature about blog articles and interviews is that they will generally link directly to your book's sales page, and also to your business website. This can give you a nice spike in sales and traffic, and can help generate ongoing leads for your business.

SPECIAL ONLINE NETWORKS FOR AUTHORS

In the early days of the Internet, authors gathered online to socialize, share information on marketing and promotion, and to promote each other's books. Many of those older sites no longer exist, because writers have moved on to established platforms like Facebook. These groups tend to come and go. To find the current active groups, search on Facebook for writer's communities that are open to the public.

For example "Writer's Group" is a public Facebook group for writers looking to mingle, meet, inform, learn, and cooperate. It has over 30,000 members. "Book & Product Promotions" is a public Facebook group created to help indie authors get their name and their work out to the masses. It has over 3,000 members. "Indie Authors International" is a public Facebook group for both readers and writers. It has over 11,000 members.

Public groups will generally add you as a member upon request. There are also private groups that you might be able to join. These can be great for networking and sharing information about the writing trade, or your particular field of expertise. Once you become active in a few public groups, you will likely find yourself invited to join the more exclusive private groups.

Once you join a group, be friendly, help other writers, and they'll help you.

SOCIAL CATALOGING SITES

Dedicate online book communities like Goodreads, Library Thing, and Shelfari are great places to get free publicity. Readers go to these sites to find new books, to chat with fellow readers, and even to interact with authors. Make sure you create an account, fill out your profile, and ad a listing for your book. Then hang out with readers and engage in discussions. The key to success with these types of sites is not to hard-sell. Become an active member of a book community, and readers will be curious about you, check out your profile, and seek out your book, website, and related products and services.

DISCUSSION BOARDS

Search for forum and discussion boards dedicated to a topic related to your book or business. Become a member, create a profile with links to your website and book page, hang out, and participate. In general, you shouldn't hard-sell in discussion groups. Instead, position yourself as an expert by answer questions and being helpful. Then people will seek out your business.

LOCAL MEET UPS

A meet-up is a chance for face-to-face contact with people who share a common interest. That interest could be the subject of your book, or even the book itself. There are meetups on almost every topic, and if you can't find one that fits your book, set up your own meetup and invite like-minded souls. These in-person meetings could lead to great word of mouth, and more free publicity down the road.

BOTTOM LINE

The Internet opens up a lot of channels for you to get free publicity for your book, but don't forget old media. They need content, too, and you never know what you'll get until you ask.

Approach top influencers, but don't be afraid to start small and build from there. The important thing is to take action, and get the word out. It will take some effort at the beginning, but once you get the free publicity ball rolling, and get some initial online exposure, people will start approaching you, begging for you to appear on their shows.

[6]

The Money Is In the List?

The Roman Emperor and philosopher Marcus Aurelius once wrote:

"The secret of all victory lies in the organization of the non-obvious."

In other words, the people who succeed in business, war, or life are those who are able to think differently and do what others aren't doing or willing to do.

If you pay attention to the world you would find that most people are playing a very unrewarding game called "Follow the follower", and similar holds in the publishing space, most authors are doing what most other authors are doing which is –Not much in terms of creativity and building a brand.

If you want to avoid the fate of most authors who sell less than 100 books a year on the front end and have no system or way of monetizing the book on the back end, then you're going to need to do what 99% of them are not doing.

The key to the success of your business is to build a strong audience. Writing a book is the easiest way to build and grow your audience. Remember your network determines your net worth. Building an email list is building your network, but what determines your success is not the list but your relationship with the list. "The money is in the relationship".

EMAIL MARKETING:

A marketing channel is any avenue or outlet that lets you promote a message to your target market. Done the right way, your book can consistently put your message, product or service in front of the appropriate audience.

You do this by using your book to build an email marketing list. Email is an amazing way to stay in touch with your audience and grow a relationship with them

And if I asked you to name the BEST traffic source online, what would you say?

Is it Facebook?
Google ads?
PPV?
PPC?

If I had to choose just ONE, I'd go with...
None of the above.

That's because hands down, my favorite traffic source is EMAIL.

The direct marketing association says over $40 for every $1 spent on email comes back in return to the business. We know that communication through email works. A recent study showed that 75% of people say they prepare for brands to communicate to them by email. Over 66.6% of people say they have purchased an item triggered by an email message sent to them. A trigger is anything that initiates an action. The most powerful trigger you, as an author, can actually use, is email. But by sending people to iBook, Chapters & Indigo, Google play or Amazon, you lose out on getting the reader's direct contact information (i.e.) email address, which means you lose out on the ability to trigger an action in your reader in the future, which ultimately leads to fewer sales and a lower customer lifetime value.

Getting an email address means you can initiate a trigger, which means more sales and a higher Customer Lifetime Value (CLV).

For any business, customers are your life blood. Writing a book will give you access to most people that might otherwise not welcome you or your business.

Understand this; if you want to make a living from your writing, if you want to exponentially grow your business or build your brand, you need to increase CLV, which means you need to actively build a direct relationship through email with your readers.

CALL TO ACTION: THE SECRET FORMULA:

Writing a book gives you a unique opportunity to connect with your readers and ask for the one thing that would make you far more sophisticated than most authors –An email lead.

HOW DO YOU GET AN EMAIL LEAD?

Well an ancient script says:

"Ask and you shall be given".

The secret is to ask, but before you ask make sure you first give something of additional value – A free report perhaps, a free video course, a free consultation, or my favorite –give your book out for free. Whatever you decide to go with, just give a compelling op-tin offer. The number 1 reason statically why people sign up for email list is because they are expecting to receive some sort of free value from you.

In the words of Gary Vaynerchuk: Jab, Jab, Jab, right Hook; give, give, give more value and then ask.

Place your optin offer strategically throughout your book; it's a great idea to use various optin offers to see what your readers connect with more.

With an email list, you can promote and share your next book idea, products, and services and you can direct email readers to your business, offers or a place where they can make a purchase.

No other service (not even social media) is as personal as email, and if done right, you'll sell way more books and grow your business exponentially through email than you could any other way.

[7]

How to Rank On Google without a Website

It doesn't matter if you are an author or a preacher! If you want to double your business and reach your clients in this era, you need to be visible online. Understand that we are living in a completely new world. The "entire" information in the world has now been made available online and people are increasingly lazy. What does this mean for you Mr. Entrepreneur?

People are more than ever before trusting google to tell them where to go for information, where to go to get help, where to go to spend their money. Worse of all, they are not willing to search pass the "first page of solution" Google offers. Now if you do not have a solid presence online, someone else does then they are getting all of your potential clients. As a matter of fact if you or your business is not ranked or visible on the first page of a google search for your niche, you could be losing as much as 70% of potential clients.

Today it's not just having a webpage, it takes more than that, you need to understand SEO and how they work and make sure your content is arranged in such a way search engines understand, you need to understand what it takes to rank on the first page of these search engines because frankly that's where all the financial exchanges takes pace. I am yet to meet the client that does business with companies listed on the 4th page of Google.

The Bottom line is this; if you truly want to grow your business at an exponential rate you need to pay attention to your visibility online.

SEO: WHAT YOU NEED TO KNOW:

SEO stands for "Search Engine Optimization". This is the process of getting your content arranged to improve the visibility for search engines. Sometimes it's simply a matter of making sure your content is arranged in a way that search engines understand. You want to do this so these search engines algorithm can easily rank your "information" in the overall database, based on several criteria's one of which is relevance. There are many parts to SEO, from the words used on your content to the way other sites link to you on the internet.

WHY SHOULD YOU CARE?

Frankly you shouldn't. Except if you are passionate about what you currently do and are looking to reach as many people as can benefit from your product or service. Search engines are indispensable to the growth of your business and brand in that they provide targeted traffic. Your potential clients at this very moment are searching for what you currently have to offer but if search engines cannot find your information or content, you will miss out on incredible opportunities to drive traffic to your site. Research has shown that search engine traffic can make or break an organization's success. Targeted traffic to your brand can provide exposure and revenue like no other channel of marketing can.

MY TOP-SECRET SEO STRATEGY

Before I go any further here, I just want you to think for a moment how many publishers you know of, that understand concepts like this and how to market your book to help you grow your business?

This is really one of our Top-Secrets here at Couronne Publishing.

Now before I go into the strategy, let's talk briefly on SEO. Remember I said part of what these search engine algorithm does is to take note of the way other sites link to you on the internet.

Backlink or Inbound link is the term used to refer to this process. This linking between your content and the content from another webpage is very important to the search engine in determining the popularity and or importance of your web information. Search engines like Google will consider web pages with more backlinks especially those from authority sites like Amazon more relevant in search results.

If you've been using search engines like Google for any amount of time I'm sure you've noticed that the same websites always tend to rank on the first page. Websites like Amazon, YouTube, Facebook, Wikipedia, etc. This is because they are regarded as High Authority websites. Having your content on these high authority sites not only gets you high authority backlinks but can also help you rank that content higher on search engines because you get to borrow their credibility, this makes you more competitive online and thereby giving you access to a massive new audience.

WHY SHOULD YOU WRITE A BOOK?

A book allows you to place your content on high authority websites that you otherwise cannot get your direct content into and leverage their credibility –Websites like Amazon, Google, Apple, etc. This helps you to rank way more easily on search engines and drives huge traffic to your brand.

Imagine if you may, having your book available on the Amazon, Google and Apple platforms also having your book trailer on YouTube, a few short articles about your book, your book listing all on LinkedIn, and an author page on Facebook, Goodreads and on Amazon author central. These are all High Authority websites, if you rank for the same keyword or key phrase, you can earn multiple spots on the first page of Google because of all the combined credibility of these sites.

My team and I have successfully done this for multiple clients. Why not you?

Having your content on the first page of a search engine like Google gives you massive visibility, and sets you apart subconsciously to potential customers as a credible leader in your niche. It also drives your competitors down in the rankings. Imagine what that could do for your brand.

[8]

The Automatic Referral Machine

Referrals are the #1 source of new business. Estimates by the experts in this field reveal that referrals are responsible for 65% of new business each year and referrals are 4 times more likely to end up as a customer. That means that all other advertising accounts for just 35% of new business.

For his book The Referral Engine, John Jantsch polled several thousand business owners. He asked 2 questions amongst others:

1. What percentage of your business comes from referrals?

2. Do you have a system for getting referrals?

He found out that 63% said they get more than half of their new business from referrals and yet 79.9% said they have no systems for getting referrals.

8 out of 10 business people are "hoping" they get enough referrals to keep their business growing. They have no system or products to serve as a catalyst to accelerate the referral process.

It's pretty obvious, there's a huge opportunity here for virtually any entrepreneur to potentially double their business by increasing their referrals. It is so much easier to do business with a referral than with a cold prospect. This is primarily because a referred prospect already thinks of you as credible and trustworthy.

So why do so very few people take advantage of this "gold mine?"

In our own research, business owners admit that the #1 reason they don't get more referrals is that they just don't know how to ask. No one likes to be sold or likes the "sales man" (however people love to buy) and asking for a referral, "stinks of salesmanship."

The typical scenario with a referral is that if I'm referring you to my friend Sally, you're going to end up in a sales meeting with Sally.

It's hard for a client to send a friend, family member or colleague to you, because doing so, means sending them into a sales meeting, and that's not very appealing. You could end up damaging their relationship with the person they'd like to refer to you. Also people are busy and they typically wouldn't just spontaneously refer you or your product.

The secret to turning your customers into a referral machine is to make it so easy for them to refer you. You want them to see it as something they can do with little or no effort.

The most effective way to do this is to remove the sales perception, remove the sales meeting and remove the sales man from the "referring equation". Remember you want it as easy as possible.

The #1 way and the most effective way to do this is to give out a copy of your book. The physical copy of your book is the golden key to opening up the door to referrals.

Here is how:

1. With a book, you are not perceived as a salesman. All of a sudden you become a welcomed guest. You are the individual looking to help and pass on value. A book is you packaging yourself and your services up in a way that you can be shared easily with others. A book is an easy way to get into your prospects network without them feeling like they are pressuring their family or friends.

Here is my law of effective marketing:

"Position yourself not as a salesman, but as an expert who provides solutions to those who are actively looking for what you have"

2. A book is evergreen. The value in a book last forever, this increases the retention value and relationship with your prospects. Simply put; a book gives you the opportunity to own mental real estate in your prospects world for a long-time. A physical book also is independent of other marketing channels and in my opinion is the one channel that can stand the test of time. I mean SEO rules will change online advertisements will evolve but the power of a book has stayed consistent and has lasted for generations.

3. A book is perceived as a gift; we typically don't throw gifts into the garbage and neither do we throw books in there. We give books out on birthdays, holidays and to share value with people we care about. A book can be gifted and re-gifted. If you are able to offer true value to your readers, people will willingly pass it on to their contacts. Your book will give people a way

to make the introduction to you and your product without a "sales meeting". By giving your book out as a gift, you can unlock the door to referrals right away.

Bottom line; writing a book is the single most important thing you can do to increase the referrals to your business and conversely potentially double your business. Your book is a "pre-qualification" medium to your prospects. You want to address the pain points that your prospective customer has, you want to answer all questions that typically come up in a sales meeting, you want to share solutions, and you want to give your prospects the opportunity to go deeper with you.

What is the next step they need to take to get deeper with your solution plan?

It has to really be clear and explicitly stated. Remember to deliver true value. Don't be scared to give your very best.

My mentor once told me:

"If you tell people everything you know for free, they would pay you to hear you say it to them all again."

And truth be told, you can't give it all away even if you wanted to. The more you give out, the more prime you are to receive.

[9]

Double Your Income

Writing a book is like a coin; on both sides you earn an income. One side is the Front end and the other side is the back end. The average author doesn't understand this; they think they both serve the same purpose.

Let me break it down:

FRONT END:

On the front end you earn an income with your book by meeting market demands. People buy books for a solution and or entertainment and as long as you meet these demands, you get paid a royalty (income). The average author stops here, and frankly this is just the beginning.

The 3 main purposes of your front end book are to:

1. Solve the number one, most immediate, biggest problem your prospect experiences right now. Your book must solve the big 'symptom' over their heads. Once you've worked with them to do that over a short period, then you've gained their trust and you can take them on long term plan on the back end, to really solve their deeper challenges.

2. Increase your reach: This is why we set goals to achieve the bestseller position. Not for the money, but for the exposure.

3. Positioning: Your book will help you gain credibility, authority and expert status. Your book will position you as a solution provider and if done correctly will attract your ideal prospects to you. The goal is to

grow a bigger and bigger list of individuals who have demonstrated their "quality" by investing in a book.

Writing a book on the front end is not about maximizing royalties, it's about maximum customer acquisition. In business, a customer is more valuable than a sale.

"The purpose of a customer is not to get a sale. The purpose of a sale is to get a customer." *–Dan Kennedy*

The customers are your assets. The average author doesn't understand that the value of a single customer can be maximized way past the sales of a book. As an author, you've established credibility and have generated a qualified prospect (in a position to buy) in front of you, through the purchase of your book, that's 50% of the deal closed right there.

The average author doesn't see that, instead they warm up the prospect for another business to close, and they go on looking for the next "customer". I'd like you to start really thinking about maximizing the value of a single reader.

We all 'know' that making a sale to a warm prospect is 7X more cost effective than chasing a new cold lead.
Yet, are you really doing it?

In order to maximize the life time value of a reader, we need to do three things among others:

1. Build a relationship with our readers; its starts with delivering on the value of the content of your book and then some. It should be truly remarkable and referral-worthy. Don't put together your book in the front-end products based on the price you're going to charge. Instead, put together your book based on the average lifetime value of a customer in your business.

2. Build your community and segmenting your readers based on their current needs and desires. Figure out where they are right now with their life and goals and use that to

customize your business offering to them. The interesting thing about when you build a community of likeminded individuals with a common goal, you have the opportunity to serve them even in areas that you personally are not an expert in. Welcome to affiliate marketing income through partnered offers.

3. Strategically lead them to your business; your book should provide content that leads into deeper opportunities for business with you on the back end. The content of your book should be engineered strategically to lead new customers into backend courses, events, or one on one consultation. When it comes to your front-end (customer acquiring) book, always remember the goal at hand. You're trying to acquire brand new customers at a low cost that will remain with you long-term, investing in multiple backend products and services. So, you need to make sure the entire product and experience associated with that first

product is strategically designed to accomplish that for you.

This is a simple principle but usually overlooked.

> *"Nobody who bought a drill actually*
> *wanted a drill. They wanted a hole.*
> *Therefore, if you want to sell drills, you should*
> *advertise information about making holes*
> *- NOT information about drills!" –Perry Marshall*

Just this paradigm shift in your philosophy and marketing will double your income.

BACK END:

The business of authorship is the back end. The one part no one talks about. This is the secret that leads authors to massive success. The one thing that separates the big time authors from everyone else. The back end is the more emotional side.

The 2 main purpose of your back end book is to:

1. Filter your leads. You cannot boil an ocean, neither can you serve everybody. You have to filter your leads to further attract your ideal clients. You do this by first understanding who your ideal client is, you have to define and know this person. Then you build a series of tasks and you use words that would only attract your ideal customers and repeal the others.

2. Convert your leads to clients: The way you do this is to educate your prospects and let them sell themselves on your value and becoming your client. This is where you double your income.

Your prospects don't care about your company or your product; they care about the solution your company can provide them. They care about the money, about the financial freedom, about the relief from pain, etc. Your company is just a tool, a means to an end. The minute you start understanding this, you are well on your way to double your business

Here is the bottom line: What do people really want? A hole (Solution). Your drill (Your business/product) can support them to achieve their goal of a hole, but people don't want to buy your drill because they hate been sold; but those really interested in making a hole will be willing to invest a few dollars to figure out how to create one quickly and easily (prequalification of leads).

So you get to work and write a book on "how to make a hole effectively and easily: Step-by-step guide", however inside this book it is recommended that they use your drill for optimum results (means to an end).

Now you are out of the picture, no sales pitch, just the prospect and the information (Your Book).

So what does he do? He decides to buy a drill. At this point you have built trust with him and he would much rather buy a drill from you than anyone else (Deal Closed).

What we have done here is to let the prospect sell themselves on becoming our clients. At this point they believe it was their idea.

It's like Las Vegas. The casinos are their back end product where the bulk of their income comes from; but they advertise everything but the gambling.

You read:

"What happens in Vegas stays in Vegas."

It's about the wild nights out on the strip, the huge shows, the five star restaurants, the lights, and the experience. They don't sell you on gambling. They sell you on fun, which is what you really want.

Once you get on a plane and arrive there, then the real selling starts. The casinos are everywhere; all the incentives are designed to get you to end up at the casinos with chips in your hand.

Bottom line: In order to double your income you must learn to take a prospect through this sales funnel that starts with your book. Trying to do this without a book is like Las Vegas with nothing but casino floors along the strip. Not a very appealing offer.

Why Entrepreneurs Should Self-Publish

The fact is that for about one in every tradition-ally published book; there are two self-published books in existence. Self-published books are tak-ing over the market share.

And why? Self-publishing gives you control and saves you time.

TIME:

First off let's talk about time; when you choose to work with a traditional publisher, you typically need to get your script to an agent who takes it to the various publishing houses. These publishing houses typically get hundreds of manuscripts every day and they decide who gets published and who doesn't. So your manuscript gets to join the line; you might get picked, you might not get picked, and your book doesn't actually get published until a year later. The point is this; if you have something good to say to add value to someone else, why not say it?

Why wait to get chosen? With self-publishing, you can have your book up and running on Amazon and most retailers within days, you get to choose yourself -now, and this is more valuable.

CONTROL:

As a creator, control over my art is very important. Understand that when you work with a traditional publisher you lose this. It's up to the 21 year old intern to make the decision on what you say and how you say it. Your content is controlled by the publisher, your design is controlled by the publisher and your copyrights are controlled by the publishers. What do you get in return for all this? "An Advance" – Except you are EL James you will make much more money by professionally self-publishing your book. Typically with traditional publishers you earn about 12% royalty but when you self-publish you earn up to a 70% royalty. It's not just the money from the front end royalties on the sale of your book but also on the backend special offers, foreign rights and your business packages that you can offer in your book if you control all the rights. These are things that the traditional publishers almost never go for.

MARKETING:

A traditional publisher is not even going to look at you unless you have a big responsive audience. But if you already have the audience, what do you need the traditional publisher for?

All the book distribution channels a traditional publisher can get you into, you can get into with a professionally self-published book. What most authors don't realize is ultimately, you have to do your own book marketing. Why do you think traditional publishers want to know if you have a big responsive audience? It's because they want to ensure they can make money on just your own marketing efforts. Bottom line; traditional publishers don't offer any form of special marketing or promotion for your book that a professional self-published book wouldn't.

The real comparison is not between "traditional published books" versus "self-published books". The real comparison is between "professional" versus "unprofessional" published books; believe it or not even the traditional publishers publish unprofessional books. I am yet to meet an actual reader who buys a book based on the publisher - readers don't care. However people buy books everyday based on how it looks. "Does this book look professional, or does it look reputable?"

This is one of the big things we emphasize to our clients now. It doesn't matter if you self-publish or use a traditional publisher, your book must look and feel very professional.

Getting a professionally self-published book these days is easy. You can pick the absolute best editors, design firms and marketing firms in the industry. The best people in the industry are no longer just available to the traditional publisher anymore; they are all striking out on their own and independently charging for their services.

If your goal is to have a professionally published book - better edited, better designed, better marketed, maximize royalties, and use it to grow your customer base, get consulting clients and speaking engagements, I highly recommend you professionally self-publish.

Statistics convey author satisfaction and preferences are higher with self-publishing. You, as a writer, deserve the finest results and the best experience with your writing and publishing career. I hope you consider self-publishing. The benefits are enormous.

[11]

Why not you?

"In life you are not guaranteed success, no one is; but we are all guaranteed a chance."

Life graciously gives everyone equally 24 hours in a day, gives everyone a chance to make something extraordinary of their lives. What makes the difference in how your life turns out is what you do with these chances/opportunities. Some of us are brave enough to believe in our own abilities and we are willing to take that first step outside our comfort zone in faith, while a larger majority of us end up playing second fiddle and live a life filled with doubt and worry. This is certainly where the difference is made.

Someone rightfully said:

"All growth happens outside of your comfort zone."

Writing, like any endeavor, takes courage; but it is also an excellent way of understanding that you have it in you to be the kind of hero you wish to be. A book is an amalgamation of thoughts and ideas and it actually does wonder to the confidence of the author. There was a period of time when I read a lot of books and I was in awe of the books and authors. I thought I never had it in me to remotely write anything so beautiful, so perfect, but I took a leap of faith. I wanted to test myself and when I did, I was amazed at the final piece. Frankly speaking, the thrill of completing your manuscript is something you will always cherish.

When you sit back and turn the pages of your manuscript, you feel a sense of pride through you because it is like seeing your own dreams come to life. The fact that you managed to defy the odds and you materialized your idea into something which will stay long after you are no longer here, is both satisfying and humbling.

As an author I envision 100 years from now, a young man cleaning up old office files perhaps files owned by his father or grandfather and picks up a copy of one of my books –Higher education 101, takes a look at it, dusts it and starts reading it.

Vwala! I get a chance to pass on my ideas to a new generation and a chance to live again.

If you are a speaker, when you speak, your words are only as powerful as they are heard. They remain only credible for as long as you say it. But when you write it down something happens, it gains immortality. With a book, your ideas go beyond you into countries you never thought possible, homes you can never get into legally, schools, libraries, college, and lives of individuals that would never accept you in, but will welcome your book.

Books are so important that God used one himself. God preserved his ideas for humanity in a book. If God uses a book to preserve divine knowledge how much more should we use this medium to preserve our ideas.

So why not you becoming an author?

If I can do it, surely you can. You've got the ideas, you've got the brains. You can study the plan; you can make your dreams come true. Why not you?

I'm ready to pledge my support to you becoming an author and make your dreams come true. What a time to be alive, what a time to give life to your dreams of becoming an author.

If you every got a chance to listen to any one of our publishing clients, here is what they would tell you:

"If i can do it, so can you."

It is time to take a chance on you. You can make a difference in this world; all you need is already inside of you.

In one of our recent visits to Italy, my wife and I visited the tomb of Raffaello Sanzio da Urbino the great renaissance Italian painter and architect. Inscribed on his tomb in the Pantheon were these words:

"Here lies Raphael, by whom nature herself feared to be outdone while he lived, and when he died, feared that she herself would die"

In life you are not guaranteed success, no one is; but we are all guaranteed a chance.

[12]

Bonus

As a special bonus for readers of this book, I'm offering you access to our advanced Authorship Webinar for Entrepreneurs and Business Professionals

Introducing:
"How to Easily Write, Publish and Use a Book to Grow Your Business, and Earn a Fortune"

To Access this Webinar, register your book at

www.osamedearhunmwunde.com/wabweb

Who we are

Couronne Publishing is a boutique publishing house that specifically addresses the needs and goals of entrepreneurs and business professionals who value creative freedom, visionary flexibility and achieving success as a published author.

Authors trust Couronne Publishing to provide them with superior services designed to empower and inspire them as they learn how to publish a book. One of the industry's leading publishers, Couronne Publishing takes pride in the one feature that sets us apart from other publishers: authors keep 100% royalties and have 100% creative power over their book.

How Couronne Publishing can help you succeed as a published author

- At Couronne Publishing, we would love to discuss your book idea, provide instructions on how to professionally write and publish a book, read a book in progress or manage publishing a book you have already completed.

- Have a great idea but aren't sure how to put that idea or incredible knowledge into words?
  We have a team of professional writers ready to help you develop your idea into a complete manuscript in your own words and voice. We provide writing services that cover all aspects of the book-writing and editing process.

- Couronne Publishing understands that books are also great marketing tools for conversion purposes. With this in mind, we have created a publishing master system that helped place several of our clients to the best seller lists.

At Couronne publishing, we can take you from book idea to published book: we are the best way possible for entrepreneurs and business professionals to turn their ideas and knowledge into a book that can change the world.

Our process has worked for hundreds of authors already, and we are growing fast. Our ultimate goal is to be the default publishing option for entrepreneurs and business professionals, and if we do that, we'll help create books that not only change the world - but that would never have otherwise existed.

That's really exciting to us.

For more information on how we turn your idea into a book that can change the world visit:

WWW.COURONNEPUBLISHING.COM

We are looking forward to hearing from you.

About The Author

Osamede Arhunmwunde is an international bestselling author, publishing and marketing expert.

Osamede is the creative director of Couronne Publishing, a boutique, creative publishing firm for entrepreneurs and business professionals and the creator of Authorship Academy, a self-publishing education platform and private self-publishing community.

He specializes in working with business professionals, leaders and entrepreneurs in all fields of business, challenging them to break through to their next level of success, credibility and significance with the most powerful conversion tool in the world - a published book.

He has worked with many prestigious conglomerates around the world. He has also developed powerful models and materials that give business leaders and entrepreneurs a dominating edge above their competitions; working with thousands of business leaders and entrepreneurs around the world. With the explosion of digital media he has now developed internet-based training's and has added several online products to his offering allowing him to reach a larger global audience.

To Connect with Osamede, visit: **WWW.OSAMEDEARHUNMWUNDE.COM**